page·a·day® | gallery calendar | 2026

DOG

THE TRUSTED BESTSELLER

1.3 MILLION COPIES SOLD!

Written by Sarah Brady
Design by Eric Harvey Brown
Photo research by Ken Yu

Workman Calendars may be purchased in bulk for business, educational, or promotional use. For information, please contact your local bookseller or the Hachette Book Group Special Markets Department at special.markets@hbgusa.com.

ISBN 978-1-5235-3139-4

Printed in China

Workman Calendars
Workman Publishing
Hachette Book Group, Inc.
1290 Avenue of the Americas
New York, NY 10104
pageaday.com

workman
CALENDARS

---

welcome to the **page-a-day**® | **gallery calendar**

how it works

The clear top pulls up and, when flipped over and snapped into the back at the bottom, becomes the easel.

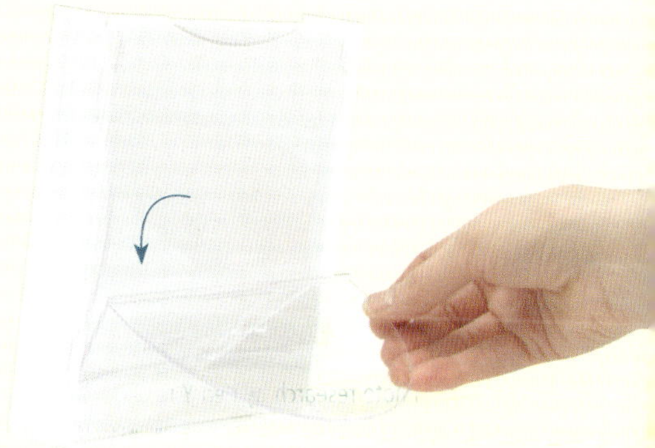

To change the date, remove the top page and slip it into the back—like taking a card off the top of a deck and putting it on the bottom.

Midway through the year, turn all the pages over, and the second half of the year begins.

Check to see if your community recycles polystyrene through a curbside program.

Workman Calendars

Don't just count the days. Make the days count.

photo credits

cover: Seregraff/Shutterstock.com

Alamy: Arco/G. Lacz 6/26, Swapan Banik 1/31–2/1, Mark J. Barrett 7/6, 8/3, LEE BEEL 11/25, Andrew Berezovsky 2/11, Cavan Images 1/9, 1/12, 1/15, 1/24–25, 1/27, 2/13, 2/16, 2/21–22, 3/25, 4/9, 4/13, 5/13, 6/17, 7/11–12, 7/25–26, 9/9, 9/10, 9/18, 9/29, 10/21, 11/13, 12/1, 12/3, Nikola Cedikova 3/23, 11/10, cfoto/YAY Media AS 1/13, Jaromír Chalabala 11/6, Johan De Meester 10/12, Monica Doallo 7/9, Farlap 5/1, 6/5, 7/17, 8/7, 9/25, 10/24–25, 11/5, 11/27, Volodymyr Finoshkin 8/21, Carolyn Franks 2/19, O. Giel 12/12–13, Jarib Gonzalez 11/17, VANESSA GROSSEMY 3/27, 7/31, Wayne HUTCHINSON 2/18, Imagebroker 5/6, Tjasa Janovljak 12/24, Juniors Bildarchiv 3/19, 5/20, 11/23, Dzmitry Kliapitski 6/15, 6/24, Ivan Kmit 8/22–23, Ekaterina Kobalnova 9/12–13, Hans Kuczka 10/16, G. Lacz/Arco 11/21–22, Britt Lakin 10/20, Erik Lam 7/16, Katie Lawlor 5/23–24, Life on white 1/14, 7/7, 10/7, Evandro Lima 11/24, Jeremy Lips 4/22, Doug loneman 8/1–2, MadeleinWolf 9/23, Tomas Maracek 5/7, Katho Menden 1/3–4, Maike Müller 5/29, Irina Nedikova 1/17–18, 8/17, Nikkimeel 10/3–4, Steve Oehlenschlager 9/16, Olga Ovcharenko 12/15, 12/25, Harry Page 6/11, Denise Panyik-Dale 11/14–15, Karen Patterson 9/4, Perky Pets 2/27, 7/24, Photoschmidt 1/29, Dave Porter 1/21, Marcelino Pozo Ruiz 2/12, Luca Prestia 1/23, Petra Richli 6/27–28, R. Richter 5/8, T. Schaefer 7/2, U.Schanz 7/14, Predrag Sepelj 8/10, S. Starick 10/2, Mary H. Swift 1/6, 4/17, 6/1, 9/30, 11/12, Sergey Taran 4/30, Petra Wegner 8/31. **AWL Images:** Robert Birkby 6/22, Sylvain Cordier 9/17, Hemis 5/16–17, Anni Sommer 3/11. **Getty Images:** Airey 2/23, alberto clemares expósito 10/14, Anna-av 1/8, 2/3, 2/5, 2/6, 2/14–15, 2/25, 3/5, 3/7–8, 3/9, 3/16, 4/1, 4/8, 4/16, 4/21, 4/23, 5/9–10, 5/11, 5/25, 6/19, 6/25, 6/29, 7/1, 7/8, 7/10, 7/13, 8/8–9, 8/12, 8/18, 8/19, 9/21, 9/24, 10/22, 11/19, 12/4, 12/5–6, 12/9, 12/11, 12/19–20, 12/23, Annaartday 3/30, Jena Ardell 1/16, Su Arslanoglu 1/26, Elizabeth Beard 3/31, Eva Blanco 10/19, Brighton Dog Photography 7/22, 10/5, bydog_studio 1/10–11, Peter Cade 8/15–16, Daniel Llao Calvet 3/2, Capuski 1/7, 5/30–31, 10/10–11, Kristin Castenschiold 10/29, Cavan Images 9/3, 10/23, Anastasiia Cherniavskaia 8/5, Kristina Chizmar 12/16, Andrew Cook 4/4–5, Cornutus 7/30, Martina Cross 9/2, Kimberly Dertinger 8/25, Catherine Falls Commercial 1/20, Peter M. Fisher 10/1, craig Fordham 4/7, fotografixx 1/2, GlobalP 5/18, 7/20, 7/29, 8/4, 9/7, 10/15, 11/11, 11/18, Elena Grigorovich 1/30, Iantfoto 10/26, IzaLysonArts 1/28, 2/2, 2/4, 2/26, 2/28–3/1, 3/13, 4/2, 4/3, 4/11–12, 4/14, 4/15, 4/20, 4/27, 5/4, 5/22, 5/26, 5/27, 6/3, 6/8, 6/10, 6/13–14, 6/23, 7/15, 7/21, 7/23, 7/28, 9/26–27, 10/13, 10/17–18, 10/28, 11/4, 12/7, 12/17, 12/28, 12/30, 12/31, JasonDoiy 7/4–5, 10/31–11/1, JoeChristensen 4/29, Henri Karppinen 1/5, Hillary Kladke 6/20–21, Kosamtu 10/06, Anita Kot 3/14–15, 7/18–19, 8/26, 9/22, LindaE 9/8, Bogdan Malizkiy 3/17, alfonso maseda Varela 2/9, meaghanbrowning 2/7–8, 3/21–22, 9/5–6, MirasWonderland 8/14, Nataba 4/25–26, Omica Photography 2/20, opalfideli 6/2, Primorac91 5/19, Alexander Pytskiy 8/6, 9/19–20, Petra Richli 3/4, 5/21, 11/28–29, 12/14, Alexandra Robins 3/10, Laurie Rubin 1/1, s5iztok 10/8, Vincent Scherer 11/7–8, Sandra Schmid 2/24, 9/14, Chris Stein 12/8, 12/10, StephanieFrey 11/26, THEPALMER 8/30, Nynke van Holten 1/22, 6/18, Oleksandra Vyshnova 9/15, Wavetop 11/20, whitebalance.oatt 8/28, Oscar Wong 2/17, xxmmxx 11/9, 11/16, Gorkem Yorulmaz 10/30. **Kim Levin:** 5/15. **Mark Rogers Photography:** 1/19, 2/10, 3/2, 3/18, 3/24, 4/10, 4/28, 5/5, 5/12, 6/6–7, 6/16, 8/11, 8/13, 8/20, 9/1, 9/11, 9/28, 10/9, 10/27, 11/2, 11/3, 12/2, 12/21, 12/22, 12/26–27. **Minden Pictures:** Mark Taylor 3/6, 3/12, 4/6, 4/18–19, 4/24, 5/2–3, 5/14, 5/28, 6/4, 6/9, 6/30, 7/3, 7/27, 8/24, 8/27. **Shutterstock.com:** Inna Astakhova 3/20, Vicente Barcelo Varona 12/18, Aleksey Boyko 3/28–29, GPPets 6/12, Eric Isselee 11/30, Neil Lockhart 3/26, Dorottya Mathe 12/29.

1 THURSDAY
JANUARY 2026

NEW YEAR'S DAY

This pup's roguish look says, "I double-dog dare you to make me get off this bed."

31 THURSDAY
DECEMBER 2026

"Keep your eyes on the stars,
but don't forget that your feet
are necessarily on the earth."
—Theodore Roosevelt

2 FRIDAY
JANUARY 2026

BANK HOLIDAY (SCT & NZ)

Research shows that dogs are more likely to beg if they make eye contact with a human—even if they're being scolded!

30 WEDNESDAY
DECEMBER 2026

May we all be blessed
with the delight of a Corgi
puppy bounding through
a winter wonderland.

3 SATURDAY
JANUARY 2026

4 SUNDAY
JANUARY 2026

"Friendship is always a sweet responsibility."
—Kahlil Gibran

29 TUESDAY
DECEMBER 2026

The plush, high-maintenance coat of the Havanese is the reason the breed is nicknamed the Spanish Silk Poodle.

5 MONDAY
JANUARY 2026

A few snowflakes are nothing to a Sheltie; the breed hails from the desolate Shetland Islands in northern Scotland.

28 MONDAY
DECEMBER 2026

Ice all around—including in the piercing gaze of this pup who's ready for a nap in front of the fire.

6 TUESDAY
JANUARY 2026

A Great Dane shows off his sass with a flawless side-eye.

26 SATURDAY DECEMBER 2026

KWANZAA BEGINS
BOXING DAY

27 SUNDAY DECEMBER 2026

A Powderpuff Chinese Crested flaunts her natural fur boots.

7 WEDNESDAY
JANUARY 2026

ORTHODOX CHRISTMAS

If a dog rolls onto his back around you, be honored—it's a vulnerable position and means he trusts you!

25 FRIDAY
DECEMBER 2026

CHRISTMAS

Three Beagles whose expressions say it all: "Let's skip the photos and get to the presents!"

8 THURSDAY
JANUARY 2026

The aristocratic look of this Saluki shows why the breed was nicknamed the Royal Dog of Egypt.

24 THURSDAY
DECEMBER 2026

A panicked Maltese poses a question: "So you're telling me he *knows* if I've been good or bad?"

9 FRIDAY
JANUARY 2026

Life lesson from an Aussiedoodle: Always take stock of your surroundings before starting your journey.

23 WEDNESDAY
DECEMBER 2026

If this German Shepherd had an online dating profile, we'd be swiping right.

10 SATURDAY
JANUARY 2026

11 SUNDAY
JANUARY 2026

A coiffed and coquettish Maltipoo using all the tricks in her book to get a treat.

22 TUESDAY
DECEMBER 2026

A black-and-white puppy gets festive, embracing the magic of the holiday season.

12 MONDAY
JANUARY 2026

Two terrier-mix pups split up the watch—one keeps an eye out ahead, and one guards the rear.

21 MONDAY
DECEMBER 2026

"What's that I hear?
The rustle of a bag
of treats being opened?"

13 TUESDAY
JANUARY 2026

Dogs have a network of veins that keeps their temperature stable by recirculating cold blood.

19 SATURDAY
DECEMBER 2026

20 SUNDAY
DECEMBER 2026

Even the most serious of humans would be reduced to baby talk when faced with this dangerously cute puppy.

14 WEDNESDAY
JANUARY 2026

Airedales were bred as rat and otter hunters—their long, stiff legs helped them jump across streams without wading.

18 FRIDAY
DECEMBER 2026

An inquisitive Yorkie is ready to tackle the future one paw at a time.

15 THURSDAY
JANUARY 2026

LAILAT AL-MIRAJ BEGINS AT SUNDOWN

A roly-poly Bulldog takes the Pokémon approach to bubbles: Gotta catch 'em all!

17 THURSDAY
DECEMBER 2026

"There is no happiness like that of being loved by your fellow-creatures."
—Charlotte Brontë

16 FRIDAY
JANUARY 2026

A curious Beagle peers out the window—is that the weekend approaching?

16 WEDNESDAY
DECEMBER 2026

To a water-loving Labrador Retriever, every splash is pure joy.

17 SATURDAY
JANUARY 2026

18 SUNDAY
JANUARY 2026

No matter how much you practice for your passport photo . . . it always comes out looking like a mug shot.

15 TUESDAY
DECEMBER 2026

Heterochromia—having two different-colored eyes—is a common condition among Siberian Huskies.

19 MONDAY
JANUARY 2026

MARTIN LUTHER KING JR. DAY (US)

A dog's field of view spans 240 degrees (compared to a human's 180), giving them a wide-angle view of the world.

14 MONDAY DECEMBER 2026

A pup dons a doleful "this must be a joke" look when faced with an empty bowl two minutes past dinner.

20 TUESDAY
JANUARY 2026

Greyhounds are surprisingly lazy; they're nicknamed the World's Fastest Couch Potato.

12 SATURDAY
DECEMBER 2026

13 SUNDAY
DECEMBER 2026

Bluey, an Australian Cattle Dog who lived to be over 29 years old, holds the Guinness World Record for oldest dog.

21 WEDNESDAY
JANUARY 2026

Dalmatians are born with plain white fur; their spots start to appear when they are around two weeks old.

11 FRIDAY
DECEMBER 2026

A Miniature Poodle rocks the asymmetrical look.

22 THURSDAY
JANUARY 2026

"[Dogs] possess many qualities humans often suppress because our lives get too busy." —John Reardon

10 THURSDAY
DECEMBER 2026

Playtime is serious business for the Russell Terrier, a breed in perpetual motion.

23 FRIDAY
JANUARY 2026

Each day is a fresh start:
As this pup reminds us,
it's best to dive right in!

9 WEDNESDAY
DECEMBER 2026

Salukis are from the Middle East; Arab tribesmen called the breed *el hor*, or "the noble."

24 SATURDAY
JANUARY 2026

25 SUNDAY
JANUARY 2026

Boxers have a youthful energy; the breed is often called the Peter Pan of dogs.

8 TUESDAY
DECEMBER 2026

"Because of the dog's joyfulness, our own is increased. It is no small gift."
—Mary Oliver

26 MONDAY
JANUARY 2026

AUSTRALIA DAY (AUS)

All Cavalier owners know the struggle of keeping their dogs' ears out of their food bowls.

7 MONDAY
DECEMBER 2026

Snowflakes all around, eyes squeezed tight, this Shiba Inu is already dreaming of warmer days.

27 TUESDAY
JANUARY 2026

A wise, white-muzzled terrier embodying the motto "Live life in full bloom."

5 SATURDAY
DECEMBER 2026

6 SUNDAY
DECEMBER 2026

Serenity: falling asleep to the gentle lapping of lake waves with your pup snuggled at your side.

28 WEDNESDAY
JANUARY 2026

Dark eye rims, aka puppy eyeliner, help absorb the sunlight that reflects off snow and ice.

4 FRIDAY
DECEMBER 2026

HANUKKAH BEGINS AT SUNDOWN

Everyone knows about trolls under bridges—but what about shepherds standing guard on boardwalks?

29 THURSDAY
JANUARY 2026

This Rottweiler knows the power he holds: a perfect head tilt that renders all humans defenseless.

3 THURSDAY
DECEMBER 2026

A pink-nosed Bull Terrier checks out last night's snowfall.

30 FRIDAY
JANUARY 2026

The average adult dog requires about 14 hours of sleep a day—a good reason to let sleeping dogs lie.

2 WEDNESDAY
DECEMBER 2026

Boxers are high-energy dogs with a playful, clownish spirit and boundless enthusiasm.

31 SATURDAY
JANUARY 2026

1 SUNDAY
FEBRUARY 2026

BLACK HISTORY MONTH BEGINS (US)

A Pekingese soaks up the last rays of the weak winter sun.

1 TUESDAY
DECEMBER 2026

Bath time is unavoidable, but this terrier is still hoping for a miracle.

2 MONDAY
FEBRUARY 2026

A little snow can't stop this sight hound from finding joy in every stride.

30 MONDAY
NOVEMBER 2026

A Pointer mix with a bad case of bed head stares gamely ahead: Monday, do your worst!

3 TUESDAY
FEBRUARY 2026

This clingy Vizsla keeps a close eye on her owner, earning the breed's "Velcro Dog" nickname.

28 SATURDAY NOVEMBER 2026

29 SUNDAY NOVEMBER 2026

This hound is proof that "personal space" is not really a concept that dogs understand.

4 WEDNESDAY
FEBRUARY 2026

Happiness is having a partner in crime.

27 FRIDAY
NOVEMBER 2026

The Airedale Terrier hails from England, where the breed was prized as a rodent hunter.

5 THURSDAY
FEBRUARY 2026

A Pug puppy turns on the charm: Just one look from those big, round eyes and we're toast!

26 THURSDAY
NOVEMBER 2026

THANKSGIVING (US)

Thankful for the unconditional love that dogs bring into the world.

6 FRIDAY
FEBRUARY 2026

WAITANGI DAY (NZ)

Despite the name and large size, the Giant Schnauzer is not a true "giant" dog breed, like the Great Dane.

25 WEDNESDAY
NOVEMBER 2026

No wallflower here! A brown-haired terrier steals the spotlight with her mischievous charm.

7 SATURDAY
FEBRUARY 2026

8 SUNDAY
FEBRUARY 2026

A group photo goes awry: "Did someone say *cheese*? Where?!"

24 TUESDAY
NOVEMBER 2026

Electrifyingly cute—
a ruffled Maltese in a
split second of repose.

9 MONDAY
FEBRUARY 2026

Gazing into the unknown,
ready for a great new
adventure . . . or just
a quick squirrel chase.

23 MONDAY NOVEMBER 2026

"Hay there . . . any chance I can get a few extra treats?"

10 TUESDAY
FEBRUARY 2026

According to Welsh legend, fairies rode Corgis into battle, explaining why some have dark fur that forms a "saddle."

21 SATURDAY
NOVEMBER 2026

22 SUNDAY
NOVEMBER 2026

A kiss from a Cane Corso is a slobbery affair . . . but these two don't seem to mind!

11 WEDNESDAY
FEBRUARY 2026

That icy stare melts away as soon as you say the magic words: "Wanna go for a walk?"

20 FRIDAY
NOVEMBER 2026

Jumping for joy literally and figuratively—it's Friday!

12 THURSDAY
FEBRUARY 2026

"No better feeling than earning a dog's trust, is there?"
—Chris Evans

19 THURSDAY
NOVEMBER 2026

An Ibizan Hound, exuding otherworldly grace, seems to float above the cratered terrain.

13 FRIDAY
FEBRUARY 2026

A scruffy white puppy with a big red rose and a whole lot of love to give.

18 WEDNESDAY
NOVEMBER 2026

Fluffed to perfection, this Sheltie nails her headshot.

14 SATURDAY
FEBRUARY 2026

15 SUNDAY
FEBRUARY 2026

VALENTINE'S DAY

Two short-haired sight hounds are about to have a real-life *Lady and the Tramp* moment.

17 TUESDAY
NOVEMBER 2026

A Bichon Frise takes a quick breather, basking in the late-autumn sunlight.

16 MONDAY
FEBRUARY 2026

PRESIDENTS DAY (US)
FAMILY DAY (CAN)
LUNAR NEW YEAR'S EVE

Dogs' whiskers, called vibrissae, send messages to their brains and help them detect environmental changes.

16 MONDAY
NOVEMBER 2026

Dogs pant to cool themselves down, but they also pant when excited or stressed.

17 TUESDAY
FEBRUARY 2026

LUNAR NEW YEAR
RAMADAN
BEGINS AT SUNDOWN

Special delivery! Who says you can't buy happiness?

14 SATURDAY
NOVEMBER 2026

15 SUNDAY
NOVEMBER 2026

Naptime: ~~hands~~ paws down the best time of day.

18 WEDNESDAY
FEBRUARY 2026

ASH WEDNESDAY

An intrepid Chihuahua checks out his snowy surroundings.

13 FRIDAY
NOVEMBER 2026

"The time to be happy is now; the place to be happy is here."
—Robert G. Ingersoll

19 THURSDAY
FEBRUARY 2026

Wide eyes and raised ears show this pup's panic when confronted by the camera—which side is her good side?

are you enjoying your page-a-day® gallery calendar?

a reminder: Now's the time to buy your DOG GALLERY CALENDAR for 2027.

In addition, you might also enjoy—or enjoy giving as a gift—another Page-A-Day® Gallery Calendar such as *Art*, *Cat*, *Audubon Nature*, or *Shoes*. These and dozens of other entertaining, enlightening, passionate titles are available wherever calendars are sold.

For a complete listing of Workman calendars, please visit **pageaday.com**.

Order a Page-A-Day® Gallery refill pack without the plastic backer at **pageaday.com/pages/gallery-refill-packs** or wherever books are sold, or call 800-759-0190 for more information.

20 FRIDAY
FEBRUARY 2026

"Dogs make me feel how shabby most of our loyalties are, how limited our patience." —Kay Francis

12 THURSDAY
NOVEMBER 2026

A Catahoula with laser focus surveys her territory.

21 SATURDAY
FEBRUARY 2026

22 SUNDAY
FEBRUARY 2026

Weekend forecast: 100 percent chance of coziness.

11 WEDNESDAY
NOVEMBER 2026

VETERANS DAY (US)
REMEMBRANCE DAY (CAN)

"Is this close-up giving me a case of googly eyes? Be honest."

23 MONDAY
FEBRUARY 2026

The neighbors might not be too happy about this Golden Retriever's mastery of "fetch the paper."

10 TUESDAY
NOVEMBER 2026

What kind of dog eats with his paws? *They all do. I haven't seen a single dog remove its paws before eating.*

24 TUESDAY
FEBRUARY 2026

Every muscle taut, a Belgian Malinois assesses a threat in the distance.

9 MONDAY
NOVEMBER 2026

The Belgian Malinois gets its Maligator nickname from the breed's ability to bite—and hold on—on command.

25 WEDNESDAY
FEBRUARY 2026

A Russell Terrier and a Toller are a study in opposites: early bird and night owl.

7 SATURDAY
NOVEMBER 2026

8 SUNDAY
NOVEMBER 2026

DIWALI BEGINS

A Rottweiler mix with joie de vivre in spades.

26 THURSDAY
FEBRUARY 2026

What do you get when you cross a snowman and a dog?
Frostbite.

6 FRIDAY
NOVEMBER 2026

Underneath its intimidating appearance, this Cane Corso's spirit is as soft and sweet as its velvety, fawn-colored coat.

27 FRIDAY
FEBRUARY 2026

Sprinter Usain Bolt runs 100 meters in 9.58 seconds—but a Greyhound can run the same distance in 5.33 seconds.

5 THURSDAY
NOVEMBER 2026

Dogs' intelligence is equivalent to that of a two-year-old human.

28 SATURDAY
FEBRUARY 2026

1 SUNDAY
MARCH 2026

WOMEN'S HISTORY MONTH BEGINS (US)

Two shepherds and a collie race down a country road, leaving clouds of icy breath in their wake.

4 WEDNESDAY
NOVEMBER 2026

A Whippet takes a rare breather. One second from now, those leaves will be dust under his feet!

2 MONDAY
MARCH 2026

LABOUR DAY
(WA AUS)

A dog's loyalty is a bond that remains unbroken—no matter the distance or time apart.

3 TUESDAY
NOVEMBER 2026

ELECTION DAY (US)

Double the cuddles—
two pups nestled in
a cozy naptime embrace.

3 TUESDAY
MARCH 2026

HOLI
BEGINS AT SUNDOWN

Frenchies overtook Labs in 2022 as the most popular breed in the United States.

2 MONDAY NOVEMBER 2026

Siberian Huskies experienced a surge of popularity after *Game of Thrones* featured the look-alike Direwolf.

4 WEDNESDAY
MARCH 2026

Look on the bright side . . .
we made it through Monday
and Tuesday already.

31 SATURDAY
OCTOBER 2026

HALLOWEEN

This Goldendoodle is all treats, no tricks!

1 SUNDAY
NOVEMBER 2026

NATIVE AMERICAN HERITAGE MONTH BEGINS (US)

DAYLIGHT SAVING TIME ENDS (US & CAN)

5 THURSDAY
MARCH 2026

Some dog breeds, like the Pharaoh Hound, have ear shapes designed to amplify sound.

30 FRIDAY
OCTOBER 2026

Fluffy white curls—
and a heart of gold
(metaphorically speaking).

6 FRIDAY
MARCH 2026

No one could have predicted that this little fluff ball would be equal parts mischief and sweetness.

29 THURSDAY
OCTOBER 2026

A Golden Retriever reminds us to take time for the simple joy of playing in a leaf pile.

7 SATURDAY
MARCH 2026

8 SUNDAY
MARCH 2026

DAYLIGHT SAVING TIME BEGINS
(US & CAN)

We wouldn't call this pup "lost" . . . just navigationally challenged.

28 WEDNESDAY
OCTOBER 2026

A Chow Chow mix who just wants to blend in with the herd.

9 MONDAY
MARCH 2026

LABOUR DAY
(VIC AUS)

A majestic Tibetan Mastiff with a shampoo commercial–worthy mane.

27 TUESDAY
OCTOBER 2026

"Life is like a mirror. Smile at it and it smiles back at you."
—Peace Pilgrim

10 TUESDAY
MARCH 2026

The art of begging: irresistible eyes plus unwavering willpower.

26 MONDAY
OCTOBER 2026

LABOUR DAY (NZ)

Two dogs, two different approaches to Monday: One's wagging, one's dragging.

11 WEDNESDAY
MARCH 2026

If this Sheltie had been at the *Barbie* casting call, Margot Robbie wouldn't have stood a chance.

24 SATURDAY
OCTOBER 2026

25 SUNDAY
OCTOBER 2026

Captivated by a squirrel, or plotting world domination? We're not sure.

12 THURSDAY
MARCH 2026

Meet the Bedlington Terrier: a bundle of energy and mischief wrapped in lamblike white curls.

23 FRIDAY
OCTOBER 2026

"There are always flowers for those who want to see them."
—Henri Matisse

13 FRIDAY
MARCH 2026

No Friday-the-13th bad luck stands a chance against this Beagle's charm!

22 THURSDAY
OCTOBER 2026

Guess which of these pups spends more time at the groomer!

14 SATURDAY
MARCH 2026

15 SUNDAY
MARCH 2026

MOTHERING SUNDAY (UK)

Luxury is a velvety, wrinkly puppy snuggled into a butter-soft cashmere throw.

21 WEDNESDAY
OCTOBER 2026

A Corgi's eyes reflect the fallen leaves, proving that beauty is in the eye of the beholder.

16 MONDAY
MARCH 2026

Wide eyes, perky ears,
every muscle tensed—
someone must have
opened the treat jar.

20 TUESDAY OCTOBER 2026

A Coton de Tulear gets comfy in a clawfoot tub—hey, that pristine white coat requires lots of upkeep.

17 TUESDAY
MARCH 2026

ST. PATRICK'S DAY

Irish Setters are famed for their glossy coats, their captivating elegance, and their gregarious personalities.

19 MONDAY
OCTOBER 2026

Safety first!
(Treats second?)

18 WEDNESDAY
MARCH 2026

When it comes to sharing toys, this pup's motto is "Finders, Keepers!"

17 SATURDAY
OCTOBER 2026

18 SUNDAY
OCTOBER 2026

Two pups sit outlined by the sun's golden glow, the picture of serenity.

19 THURSDAY
MARCH 2026

EID AL-FITR
BEGINS AT SUNDOWN

Corded coats are not just aesthetically striking—they help dogs blend in with the sheep they herd.

16 FRIDAY
OCTOBER 2026

Fluff beyond measure is man's greatest treasure . . . that's how the quote goes, right?

20 FRIDAY
MARCH 2026

This little Bullmastiff puppy is stumped by the canine version of a Rubik's Cube.

15 THURSDAY
OCTOBER 2026

What is it about the Golden Retriever that radiates sunshine and joy?

21 SATURDAY
MARCH 2026

22 SUNDAY
MARCH 2026

Let's get this paw-ty started! Bring on the treats, toys, and tail-wagging fun.

14 WEDNESDAY
OCTOBER 2026

Australian Shepherds are known for their distinctive patchwork-like merle coats.

23 MONDAY
MARCH 2026

"It is sufficient challenge for any day to live up to your dog's opinion of you."
—Robert Brault

13 TUESDAY OCTOBER 2026

A sunrise swim rejuvenates body and mind.

24 TUESDAY
MARCH 2026

This Border Terrier mix is so dignified, he even *relaxes* with poise and elegance.

12 MONDAY
OCTOBER 2026

INDIGENOUS PEOPLES' DAY (US)
THANKSGIVING (CAN)
COLUMBUS DAY (US)

Two pups as passengers? Double the cuteness . . . and double the chaos!

25 WEDNESDAY
MARCH 2026

Every gray whisker
on this dog's face tells
a tale of love, loyalty,
and a lifetime of memories.

10 SATURDAY OCTOBER 2026

11 SUNDAY OCTOBER 2026

"Dog (*noun*): A kind of additional or subsidiary Deity designed to catch the overflow and surplus of the world's worship."
—Ambrose Bierce

26 THURSDAY
MARCH 2026

Eyes bright, tongue out—
a puppy's enthusiasm
is contagious.

9 FRIDAY
OCTOBER 2026

"Are you *sure* there aren't any more treats?"

27 FRIDAY
MARCH 2026

Long ago, *hound* was used to identify any dog, while *dog* referred specifically to mastiffs and large breeds.

8 THURSDAY
OCTOBER 2026

This Bearded Collie keeps it trendy with his stylish half-up, half-down hairstyle.

28 SATURDAY
MARCH 2026

29 SUNDAY
MARCH 2026

PALM SUNDAY

"A well-spent day brings happy sleep."
—Leonardo da Vinci

are you enjoying your page-a-day® gallery calendar?

a reminder: Now's the time to buy your DOG GALLERY CALENDAR for 2027.

In addition, you might also enjoy—or enjoy giving as a gift—another Page-A-Day® Gallery Calendar such as *Art*, *Cat*, *Audubon Nature*, or *Shoes*. These and dozens of other entertaining, enlightening, passionate titles are available wherever calendars are sold.

For a complete listing of Workman calendars, please visit **pageaday.com**.

Order a Page-A-Day® Gallery refill pack without the plastic backer at **pageaday.com/pages/gallery-refill-packs** or wherever books are sold, or call 800-759-0190 for more information.

30 MONDAY
MARCH 2026

Tangled, unruly grass is no match for this Yorkie's impeccably sharp haircut.

7 WEDNESDAY
OCTOBER 2026

It's easy to see why the Saluki's elegance is often described as "haunting."

31 TUESDAY
MARCH 2026

From tiny to towering, these two prove that size is just a number in the world of canine companionship.

6 TUESDAY
OCTOBER 2026

Cuddled up with her head nestled snugly between her paws, a hound is all set for a peaceful nap.

1 WEDNESDAY
APRIL 2026

PASSOVER
BEGINS AT SUNDOWN

Calm eyes belie the Russell Terrier's true nature: a feisty firecracker always ready to explore.

5 MONDAY
OCTOBER 2026

LABOUR DAY
(ACT, NSW & SA AUS)

A white Poodle framed
by falling leaves—
a serene autumn scene.

2 THURSDAY
APRIL 2026

An adorable trio of Whippets surrounded by perfect pink tulips? Pinch us, we must be dreaming.

3 SATURDAY
OCTOBER 2026

4 SUNDAY
OCTOBER 2026

"How it is that animals understand things I do not know, but it is certain that they do understand."
—Frances Hodgson Burnett

3 FRIDAY
APRIL 2026

GOOD FRIDAY

Being so close to the forest floor allows this low-rider to appreciate all that nature has to offer.

2 FRIDAY
OCTOBER 2026

Ringing in spooky season with the little gray ghost of the canine world (also known as the Cesky Terrier).

4 SATURDAY
APRIL 2026

5 SUNDAY
APRIL 2026

EASTER

"Do these ears distract you from the fact that I ate a few dozen jellybeans this morning?"

1 THURSDAY
OCTOBER 2026

DISABILITY EMPLOYMENT AWARENESS MONTH BEGINS (US)

With a feathery fringe and stunning spotted skin, the Chinese Crested is a natural diva.

6 MONDAY
APRIL 2026

EASTER MONDAY BANK HOLIDAY
(ENG., WALES, N. IRE., AUS, NZ)

"Cuddling a dog could be as soothing to the mind and heart as deep meditation."
—Dean Koontz

30 WEDNESDAY
SEPTEMBER 2026

"I'm not sure I follow . . . what do you mean, we're done with our walk already?"

7 TUESDAY
APRIL 2026

According to this German Wirehaired Pointer, whiskers and wisteria are the perfect pairing.

29 TUESDAY
SEPTEMBER 2026

Miniature Poodles are small—just 10–15 pounds—but have a big personality.

8 WEDNESDAY
APRIL 2026

A Spanish Water Dog with a perm so good, he would give Cher a run for her money.

28 MONDAY
SEPTEMBER 2026

Dripping with jewels (okay, and a little drool, too), this Frenchie is the fanciest in all the land.

9 THURSDAY
APRIL 2026

Queen Elizabeth II was a Corgi aficionado: She owned more than 30 during her seven-decade reign.

26 SATURDAY
SEPTEMBER 2026

27 SUNDAY
SEPTEMBER 2026

Nothing detracts from these hounds' laser-sharp focus—except maybe a quick ear smooch.

10 FRIDAY
APRIL 2026

Scamp (*noun*): rascal, rogue. (We think that about sums it up for this mischievous little cutie!)

25 FRIDAY
SEPTEMBER 2026

The Bichon Frise formula:
70 percent puffball,
30 percent mischief,
100 percent lovable.

11 SATURDAY
APRIL 2026

12 SUNDAY
APRIL 2026

ORTHODOX EASTER

Golden hour is in full swing, setting an Australian Shepherd aglow among purple blooms.

24 THURSDAY
SEPTEMBER 2026

A Border Collie stares at the camera, secure in the knowledge that black and white will always be chic.

13 MONDAY
APRIL 2026

"The reason a dog has so many friends is that he wags his tail instead of his tongue."
—Anonymous

23 WEDNESDAY
SEPTEMBER 2026

Cute aggression: the overwhelming urge to squeeze something too adorable to handle.

14 TUESDAY
APRIL 2026

Easy like Tuesday morning . . . that's how the song goes, right?

22 TUESDAY
SEPTEMBER 2026

Ball in mouth, ears aloft, this Beagle has mastered the art of fetching with style.

15 WEDNESDAY
APRIL 2026

A curly-coated Poodle mix pops his head up to ask: Friend or foe?

21 MONDAY
SEPTEMBER 2026

INTERNATIONAL DAY OF PEACE

A pastel backdrop brings out hidden undertones of lavender and slate blue in the Weimaraner's gray coat.

16 THURSDAY
APRIL 2026

Why would you need to see when you look this good?

19 SATURDAY
SEPTEMBER 2026

20 SUNDAY
SEPTEMBER 2026

YOM KIPPUR
BEGINS AT SUNDOWN

Why did the dog float?
He was a good buoy!

17 FRIDAY
APRIL 2026

An alert, poised posture with weight shifted forward signifies interest—in this case, maybe a nearby squirrel.

18 FRIDAY
SEPTEMBER 2026

"A dog has nothing to do and no time to rest."
—Tamil proverb

18 SATURDAY
APRIL 2026

19 SUNDAY
APRIL 2026

He may look cute, but he's a handful: GPS tracking collars found that the Malinois was the most active breed.

17 THURSDAY
SEPTEMBER 2026

A bearlike, imposing Tibetan Mastiff with a formidable aura.

20 MONDAY
APRIL 2026

Labrador Retrievers are equally at home in water or on land, as a young Lab fresh out of a lake demonstrates.

16 WEDNESDAY
SEPTEMBER 2026

Brittanys are disciplined, confident hunting dogs in the field—and at home, they're clingy, lovable softies.

21 TUESDAY
APRIL 2026

Getting up close and personal with a peppy Collie mix.

15 TUESDAY
SEPTEMBER 2026

HISPANIC HERITAGE MONTH BEGINS (US)

This Papillon puts the "ear" in endearing!

22 WEDNESDAY
APRIL 2026

EARTH DAY

"Happiness is a nice long nap."
—Charles M. Schulz

14 MONDAY
SEPTEMBER 2026

Fur so silky soft,
you can almost feel it
through the photo.

23 THURSDAY
APRIL 2026

Dogs' ears contain pheromone-filled glands, which is why dogs often sniff each other's ears.

12 SATURDAY
SEPTEMBER 2026

13 SUNDAY
SEPTEMBER 2026

GRANDPARENTS DAY (US)

A Dachshund, a Corgi, and a Border Collie walk into a park . . .

24 FRIDAY
APRIL 2026

Black and tan: a timeless combo, and one that effortlessly emphasizes this Hovawart's soft features.

11 FRIDAY
SEPTEMBER 2026

ROSH HASHANAH
BEGINS AT SUNDOWN

The perfect layers on this Yorkie mix could serve as inspo for Jennifer Aniston's iconic *Friends* hairstyle.

25 SATURDAY
APRIL 2026

ANZAC DAY
(AUS & NZ)

26 SUNDAY
APRIL 2026

Windows down, tongue out, bandanna on: Weekend mode activated!

10 THURSDAY SEPTEMBER 2026

Dogs are one of the most diverse mammals—think of the difference between this Borzoi and a Yorkie.

27 MONDAY
APRIL 2026

A Boxer and a Rhodesian Ridgeback on an early-morning traipse through the park.

9 WEDNESDAY
SEPTEMBER 2026

With an irresistible, heart-melting expression, this pup campaigns for another treat.

28 TUESDAY
APRIL 2026

"To live at all
is miracle enough."
—Mervyn Peake

8 TUESDAY
SEPTEMBER 2026

"An inconvenience
is only an adventure
wrongly considered."
—G. K. Chesterton

29 WEDNESDAY
APRIL 2026

Frosty silver hairs dot this Rottweiler's muzzle—evidence of a life well lived.

7 MONDAY
SEPTEMBER 2026

LABOR DAY
(US & CAN)

The Whippet is called the poor man's Greyhound, with speeds of 35 miles per hour to the Greyhound's 45.

30 THURSDAY
APRIL 2026

Basenjis can be willful and independent; their personality is often described as catlike.

5 SATURDAY
SEPTEMBER 2026

Surf's up! These water-loving pups are catching some weekend waves.

6 SUNDAY
SEPTEMBER 2026

FATHER'S DAY
(AUS & NZ)

1 FRIDAY
MAY 2026

ASIAN AMERICAN AND PACIFIC ISLANDER HERITAGE MONTH BEGINS (US)

A regal Beagle guards spring's prize: ruffled, golden daffodils.

4 FRIDAY
SEPTEMBER 2026

Having a Great Dane means saying goodbye to leaving food unattended on the countertops.

2 SATURDAY
MAY 2026

3 SUNDAY
MAY 2026

Nothing soothes the soul more than a snuggle from a puppy.

3 THURSDAY
SEPTEMBER 2026

The snores emanating from this Saint Bernard could be mistaken for thunder on a rainy day.

4 MONDAY
MAY 2026

BANK HOLIDAY (UK)
LABOUR DAY (QLD AUS)

"Grow old along with me!
The best is yet to be . . ."
—Robert Browning

2 WEDNESDAY
SEPTEMBER 2026

A pair of Belgian Sheepdogs checks out the view—pink poppies as far as the eye can see.

5 TUESDAY
MAY 2026

This Chihuahua's cocked ear issues a challenge: "Bring on Tuesday."

1 TUESDAY
SEPTEMBER 2026

Dogs can wiggle each nostril independently and can determine which nostril is smelling a particular odor.

6 WEDNESDAY
MAY 2026

The Basset Hound name comes from the French for "low"—these dogs stand about a foot tall at the shoulder!

31 MONDAY
AUGUST 2026

SUMMER BANK HOLIDAY
(ENG., WALES, N. IRE.)

The Eurasier has all the classic Spitz-breed hallmarks: fox-like face, fluffy tail, and pointed ears.

7 THURSDAY
MAY 2026

Zoomies activated!

29 SATURDAY
AUGUST 2026

30 SUNDAY
AUGUST 2026

"You are wrong if you think Joy emanates only or principally from human relationships. . . . It is in everything and anything we might experience."
—Jon Krakauer

8 FRIDAY
MAY 2026

Fluffy dandelion crowns can't quite compare to the resplendent pouf atop a Bichon Frise.

28 FRIDAY
AUGUST 2026

We've heard of the "man cave" and the "she shed," but we're not so sure about this Chow Chow's "scent den."

9 SATURDAY
MAY 2026

An Australian Shepherd finds herself nap-trapped in a cozy hammock.

10 SUNDAY
MAY 2026

MOTHER'S DAY

27 THURSDAY
AUGUST 2026

"A true friend leaves paw prints on your heart."
—Anonymous

11 MONDAY
MAY 2026

Pharaoh Hounds have a unique talent—they can "blush" pink across their nose and ears when excited.

26 WEDNESDAY AUGUST 2026

“Look, Ma, no paws!”

12 TUESDAY
MAY 2026

Three little scoops of delight: the canine version of a Neapolitan cone.

25 TUESDAY
AUGUST 2026

MAWLID AN-NABI BEGINS AT SUNDOWN

As Bearded Collie enthusiasts often say, “A busy Beardie is a happy Beardie.”

13 WEDNESDAY
MAY 2026

This strawberry-blond shepherd surreptitiously scopes out a nearby dog park.

24 MONDAY
AUGUST 2026

"Awwww" is the only appropriate response to meeting a Goldendoodle, a real-life teddy bear.

14 THURSDAY
MAY 2026

"Ready for my interview. Ask me anything about fetch!"

22 SATURDAY
AUGUST 2026

23 SUNDAY
AUGUST 2026

Basking in the hot sun, a Cane Corso knows how to enjoy the weekend—horizontally!

15 FRIDAY
MAY 2026

Happy Friday! Time to unleash the weekend adventures.

21 FRIDAY AUGUST 2026

The Borzoi, with its honeyed waves and elegant stature, is the embodiment of grace.

16 SATURDAY
MAY 2026

17 SUNDAY
MAY 2026

Looking for mischief . . . and maybe a few treats along the way.

20 THURSDAY
AUGUST 2026

A Corgi's eyebrow coloring accentuates her sassy side: "You expect me to move? Good luck with that."

18 MONDAY
MAY 2026

VICTORIA DAY (CAN)

Border Collies are scary smart—they're often able to learn a new command in fewer than five attempts.

19 WEDNESDAY
AUGUST 2026

Hairless dogs like this American Hairless Terrier are vulnerable to sunburn—dog sunscreen can help.

19 TUESDAY
MAY 2026

It was a ruff day on the water for this German Wirehaired Pointer mix, but nothing a romp in the sun won't fix.

18 TUESDAY AUGUST 2026

Just like marshmallow, chocolate, and graham crackers, these three make the perfect trio—we want s'more!

20 WEDNESDAY
MAY 2026

A German Shepherd *lying down*? Take a picture, it'll last longer.

17 MONDAY
AUGUST 2026

The Shiba Inu breed is vocal; Shibas bark, yip, yodel, purr, and even scream.

21 THURSDAY
MAY 2026

Canine sleep cycles last about 45 minutes, with only 10 percent spent in REM.

15 SATURDAY
AUGUST 2026

16 SUNDAY
AUGUST 2026

Two Dalmatians search high and low for treats—and we have a feeling one of them is on the right path.

22 FRIDAY
MAY 2026

"That once in a lifetime dog . . . [is a] special bond that not everybody gets."
—Hilary Duff

14 FRIDAY
AUGUST 2026

A portrait so striking, it wouldn't be out of place in the Metropolitan Museum of Art.

23 SATURDAY
MAY 2026

24 SUNDAY
MAY 2026

Huskies race across the beach, their strides echoing the rhythm of the waves.

13 THURSDAY
AUGUST 2026

A white muzzle usually signifies age, but frosting (as it's affectionately called) can be seen in young dogs, too.

25 MONDAY
MAY 2026

MEMORIAL DAY (US)
SPRING BANK HOLIDAY (UK)

The Boston Terrier breed is a misnomer—Bostons are not in the American Kennel Club's Terrier Group.

12 WEDNESDAY AUGUST 2026

Nose to nose, two Yorkies speak a language beyond words.

26 TUESDAY
MAY 2026

EID AL-ADHA
BEGINS AT SUNDOWN

Stump? No, this is a wooden throne—just the right perch for a stately Airedale Terrier.

11 TUESDAY
AUGUST 2026

While they're usually called *puppy*-dog eyes, it's older dogs, like this hound mix, who have truly mastered the art.

27 WEDNESDAY
MAY 2026

A white retriever peers out soulfully from between magnolia blossoms.

10 MONDAY
AUGUST 2026

A Poodle with the model-off-duty look down pat.

28 THURSDAY
MAY 2026

Scientists think that dogs cock their heads to hear better—the cuteness is the cherry on top!

8 SATURDAY
AUGUST 2026

9 SUNDAY
AUGUST 2026

"Press on, take courage."
—Carlos Filipe Ximenes Belo

29 FRIDAY
MAY 2026

It's amazing that the Chow Chow's most striking feature isn't its fluffy coat but its vibrant blue-black tongue.

7 FRIDAY
AUGUST 2026

Keen-eyed and single-minded, the English Foxhound embodies centuries of hunting heritage.

30 SATURDAY
MAY 2026

31 SUNDAY
MAY 2026

A young terrier mix outperforming the competition by leaps and bounds.

6 THURSDAY
AUGUST 2026

"You must. . . launch yourself on every wave, find your eternity in each moment."
—Henry David Thoreau

1 MONDAY
JUNE 2026

LESBIAN, GAY, BISEXUAL, TRANSGENDER, QUEER, AND INTERSEX PRIDE MONTH BEGINS (US)

For years, only the Japanese imperial family and their associates were allowed to own Akitas.

5 WEDNESDAY
AUGUST 2026

An Afghan Hound embraces the dog days of summer.

2 TUESDAY
JUNE 2026

What's on deck for this spotty sailor? An afternoon of relaxing in the sun.

4 TUESDAY
AUGUST 2026

"Courage without Ferocity, and all the virtues of Man without his Vices." —Lord Byron, "Epitaph to a Dog"

3 WEDNESDAY
JUNE 2026

You could easily mistake this tawny shepherd for a sleeping fawn—if not for the perky black ears poking up.

3 MONDAY
AUGUST 2026

CIVIC HOLIDAY (CAN)
SUMMER BANK HOLIDAY (SCT)

The Bouvier des Flandres haircut—ideal for scary movies, emo concerts, and keeping sun out of your eyes.

4 THURSDAY
JUNE 2026

A cream-colored Goldendoodle, looking sharp with a summer haircut.

1 SATURDAY
AUGUST 2026

2 SUNDAY
AUGUST 2026

"Little ears, big personality": the Shar-Pei motto.

5 FRIDAY
JUNE 2026

Despite their resemblance, the Keeshond breed is about seven times the size of the Pomeranian breed.

31 FRIDAY
JULY 2026

The Great Pyrenees has an independent streak, honed over years of solitary sheep-guarding in the mountains.

6 SATURDAY
JUNE 2026

7 SUNDAY
JUNE 2026

No greater joy than a pile of puppies.

30 THURSDAY
JULY 2026

Through fur-framed eyes,
a Barbet sees the world as a
blur of endless curiosities.

8 MONDAY
JUNE 2026

A fearless Dalmatian demonstrates the determination and tenacity of the breed.

29 WEDNESDAY
JULY 2026

As this confident Lab knows, black goes with everything. Even a violent shade of violet.

9 TUESDAY
JUNE 2026

Somewhere, far in the distance, the tiniest morsel of food was dropped.

28 TUESDAY
JULY 2026

A piece of advice from a Bearded Collie—always paws before you make a move.

10 WEDNESDAY
JUNE 2026

"Puppy-dog eyes" are real—when looking at people, dogs move their eyebrow muscles, making their eyes look bigger.

27 MONDAY
JULY 2026

An all-over fringe gives this Chihuahua a permanently windswept look.

11 THURSDAY
JUNE 2026

The Irish Wolfhound: gentle when stroked, fierce when provoked.

25 SATURDAY
JULY 2026

26 SUNDAY
JULY 2026

Sun on her fur, paws in the water, a Golden Retriever follows her nose to adventure.

12 FRIDAY
JUNE 2026

Shimmering amber eyes perfectly complement this Brittany's glossy auburn fur.

24 FRIDAY
JULY 2026

Irish Wolfhounds are gentle giants, but giants all the same; males can weigh up to 180 pounds.

13 SATURDAY
JUNE 2026

14 SUNDAY
JUNE 2026

FLAG DAY
(US)

You can't keep an English Springer Spaniel from the water—they have a natural affinity for swimming.

23 THURSDAY
JULY 2026

Dogs are remarkable, shifting from couch potatoes to forest explorers in the blink of an eye.

15 MONDAY
JUNE 2026

AL-HIJRA
BEGINS AT SUNDOWN

A Beagle gives a master class in sass.

22 WEDNESDAY
JULY 2026

Your standard game of fetch or an alien abduction? We'll let you decide.

16 TUESDAY
JUNE 2026

Almost totally airborne, a Doodle nabs a Frisbee with ease.

21 TUESDAY
JULY 2026

A Poodle's golden curls, bathed in sunlight, in a field of lavender blossoms—is there anything more poetic?

17 WEDNESDAY
JUNE 2026

"Now that I've practiced guarding the house, time to move on to guarding the treat jar. Right?"

20 MONDAY
JULY 2026

Caught mid-lip curl, this Small Munsterlander does his best Blue Steel.

18 THURSDAY
JUNE 2026

What's black and white
and pink all over?
A Border Collie mix
with a bone to pick.

18 SATURDAY
JULY 2026

19 SUNDAY
JULY 2026

"People tend to forget that play is serious."
—David Hockney

19 FRIDAY
JUNE 2026

JUNETEENTH (US)

Happily, it's becoming more taboo to crop dogs' ears; here, a Doberman shows off the natural look.

17 FRIDAY
JULY 2026

Ahoy, Friday!
Time to fetch some fun!

20 SATURDAY
JUNE 2026

21 SUNDAY
JUNE 2026

FATHER'S DAY
(US, CAN, UK)

Any parent will recognize the look on this Vizsla's face—a complex mixture of love, annoyance, and pride.

16 THURSDAY
JULY 2026

Fueled by athleticism and wanderlust, Catahoulas can climb fences, making them expert escape artists.

22 MONDAY
JUNE 2026

"Want to come in? That'll cost you two biscuits and a belly rub."

15 WEDNESDAY
JULY 2026

These pups prove that a little friendly competition never hurt anybody . . . except maybe someone's pride.

23 TUESDAY
JUNE 2026

"If one truly loves nature one finds beauty everywhere."
—Vincent van Gogh

14 TUESDAY
JULY 2026

Rub-a-dub-dub, this pup
was due for a scrub!

24 WEDNESDAY
JUNE 2026

ST. JEAN BAPTISTE DAY (CAN)

The brindled coloration of black stripes on a reddish base is commonly termed tiger stripes.

13 MONDAY
JULY 2026

Early mornings aren't so bad with this mountain view!

25 THURSDAY
JUNE 2026

Sand under his paws, wind ruffling his fur—this terrier could teach us a thing or two about how to relax.

11 SATURDAY
JULY 2026

12 SUNDAY
JULY 2026

Heaven on earth: where rolling waves meet sun-soaked sand, and you feel like you can run forever.

26 FRIDAY
JUNE 2026

A sun-kissed Cavalier's button-black eyes peek out amid a sea of yellow and purple blooms.

10 FRIDAY
JULY 2026

MATARIKI (NZ)

Internet slang calls this a blep: when only a small part of a dog's tongue is sticking out.

27 SATURDAY
JUNE 2026

28 SUNDAY
JUNE 2026

"He that can take rest is greater than he that can take cities."
—Benjamin Franklin

9 THURSDAY
JULY 2026

This proud pup shows off his mane attraction.

29 MONDAY
JUNE 2026

Friends fur-ever.

8 WEDNESDAY JULY 2026

A Papillon with oversized fringed ears lives up to the breed's nickname—the Butterfly Dog.

30 TUESDAY
JUNE 2026

Tuesday: Proof that this Pointer mix survived Monday (ruffled fur and all).

7 TUESDAY
JULY 2026

We could get lost in the velvety wrinkles of these two Dogues de Bordeaux.

1 WEDNESDAY
JULY 2026

CANADA DAY
(CAN)

She is beauty, she is grace, she is just a *little* bit addicted to playing fetch.

6 MONDAY
JULY 2026

An American Pit Bull Terrier's floppy ear adds a touch of whimsy to his otherwise stoic appearance.

2 THURSDAY
JULY 2026

Alert and poised, with a leggy sort of elegance, it is easy to see why the Ibizan Hound is described as deerlike.

4 SATURDAY
JULY 2026

INDEPENDENCE DAY (US)

"[Freedom is] the last best hope of earth."
—Abraham Lincoln

5 SUNDAY
JULY 2026

it's time to flip your calendar around

Now that you've moved the July 2 page to the back of your plastic calendar holder, move this page to the back as well, then lift all the calendar pages, as a group, from the holder and flip them around. July 3 will now be on top.

To enjoy the next six months, simply continue through the year as you've been doing, moving a calendar page to the back of the stack each day.

3 FRIDAY JULY 2026

This Westie mustache you a question—does he have crumbs in his beard?